Curiosity Keeps the Cat Alive

Curiosity Keeps the Cat Alive

By Kenneth M. Hekman

Copyright © 2010 by Kenneth M. Hekman
Published by Trillium Arts Press in association
with Lulu.com
All rights reserved
First edition printed 2010
Printed in the United States of America

ISBN 978-0-557-31038-8

Table of Contents

Preface

How do the best organizations get that way and stay that way? That's the question that sparked a lifetime of experimentation culminating in this book. It is a question that has intrigued leaders in business and non-profit organizations in every culture and every era. It has spawned research, dissertations, rock-star consultancies and more, but organizations everywhere still struggle to make their mark and sustain their successes.

This simple book offers a simple and intuitive explanation, not with research but with a story. The story is fictional but not without a factual basis. It is an allegory based on observations from many organizations in many settings.

It offers an explanation, but it is also designed to stimulate more meaningful questions in the heart and mind of the curious reader. Look for your own answers to your own questions, for well-designed questions can be the basis for true enlightenment.

Ken Hekman
Holland, Michigan USA
2010

Part 1: The Newbury Fable

A New Beginning

Dan Morgan jogged gracefully through the neighborhood as the morning sun cast a pink glow. He enjoyed his daily run, partly because it gave him time for quiet reflection, but also because he enjoyed the challenge of continually improving himself.

This morning he was particularly lighthearted. He was looking forward to his first meeting at noon with Kim Johnson and Sean Petrovich. Dan, Kim and Sean had recently been elected as officers of the Newbury Rotary club. Dan, as president, had called this planning meeting to set the stage for what he hoped would be a period of positive change. Membership had been declining in the past few years despite a healthy local economy, and Dan sensed that the club needed a fresh approach to leadership. Kim and Sean were each respected for their leadership abilities, but Dan didn't really know them very well. Now he would have the opportunity to get better acquainted as they worked together to make a difference for their community.

Dan was no stranger to leadership challenges in his own rite. As the CEO of Community Hospital, Dan had led a complex organization through a dramatic turnaround. When he arrived in Newbury eight years ago, Community Hospital was in dire condition. The hospital had suffered from four consecutive years of operating losses, leaving reserves depleted and employees disheartened to the point of exhaustion. The Board of Directors of the non-profit organization knew that drastic measures needed to be taken by a strong leader if the hospital were to survive. In the first few months, Dan worked day and night to earn the trust of the physicians, the staff, the board, and the community.

His diligence had paid off. Once they understood his commitment to the success of the organization, the physicians and staff rallied around his recommendations for change. The board stood back and watched as their leader introduced creative initiatives and disciplined tactics to get the job done. In just two years, the organization was back in the black. As the reserves and the credit rating grew, Dan launched a campaign for a new and vibrant urgent care facility on the north side of town to complement the main south side campus.

This morning, Dan was looking back with a deep sense of satisfaction. This was the first anniversary of the opening of the new facility. The hospital had continued to thrive under his leadership and now he was looking for an opportunity to apply those leadership skills in new directions for the benefit of the people of Newbury.

Professional Organization

With the sun at her back, Kim Johnson guided her BMW along the familiar route to East Towne Manufacturing. She was prepared for a typical day of meetings with engineers, salespeople, and managers. Kim had been President of East Towne Manufacturing for twelve years. Her background as an engineer combined with her natural abilities as a confident decision maker made her a natural choice to lead the automotive supply company. The parent company of East Towne Manufacturing was an Austrian holding company. The geographic and cultural distance required them to rely heavily on Kim to make decisions as she saw fit.

East Towne Manufacturing was a steady business in an unglamorous industry. Auto parts manufacturing had grown increasingly competitive in the past decade, but Kim's company had held its own thanks to solid engineering and precise manufacturing disciplines. East Towne Manufacturing also held a patent for a device used in fuel injection systems found in BMWs and other prestigious cars. The patented device accounted for about a quarter of East Towne Manufacturing revenues, and was not due to expire for another four years.

As Kim wheeled into her presidential parking spot, she remembered her noon meeting with the Rotary club officers. She was glad to have been nominated, and she was looking forward to bringing a degree of professionalism and organization to the club. She had been periodically annoyed at the previous officers' lack of preparation for some of the meetings. On occasion, speakers were no-shows, although the former leaders simply shrugged it off. It's about time, Kim thought, for the clubs officers to take their roles a little more seriously and respect the expectations of club members.

Big Ideas

Sean Petrovich liked being a small retailer, partly because of traditions about store hours. Sean was not a morning person, so having a Hallmark store that didn't open until 9 a.m. was a good fit for him.

Sean was enjoying his second cup of coffee on the deck of his modest Newbury home as the sun filled the woods behind his yard. He smiled as he remembered his meeting the day before with a sales representative for a new product line of gifts he was considering. Sean always enjoyed exploring new products. The annual buyer's convention was the highlight of his year. He was like a kid in a candy store walking through the exhibit area where suppliers were presenting their best ideas about what shoppers would be looking for. The next buyer's conference was a month away, and the sales rep that stopped by yesterday not only presented some exciting new products, but also gave him complementary tickets to the conference.

Sean's wife, Kathy, joined him on the deck. "Will you be coming home for lunch today?"

"No, I have my first planning meeting with the Rotary club officers today. Being a part of the club has been good for business, so I'm curious about the impact of having a higher profile. Besides, I'm eager to give something back to the community above and beyond our contributions to the club. And who knows, I can probably learn something from Dan and Kim. They are both pretty sharp leaders."

"Well Dan sure has made a difference at the hospital, and Kim runs one of the largest companies in town. If hanging around with them can help you make the store more profitable, I'm all for it."

Sean and Kathy weren't big spenders, but Kathy paid the bills, and she knew that the store was providing them only a modest living. Sean had an eye for flashy new products for the store, but some of the flashiest ideas didn't sell very well and ended up on the discount table. He advertised periodically in the local newspaper, the Newbury News, especially around the holidays, but sales would usually lag the rest of the year. She was proud of Sean for taking the risks of an entrepreneur, but she often wondered if things would be different if Sean had a stable income by working for someone else.

The Lunch Meeting

Dan settled into the corner booth at the restaurant a few minutes early to secure his favorite table for the meeting with Kim and Sean. It wasn't very busy, but he came here often because it offered a quiet spot to talk, and the food was consistently tasty even if the presentation lacked imagination. He pulled out a pad of paper and his favorite pen, ready to capture ideas that flowed from the meeting.

Kim arrived right on time, leather notepad in hand. She sat down and shook Dan's hand firmly in a single motion.

"It's good to see you, Dan," she said as she sipped her water. "I'm glad we'll have the chance to work together. I've admired what you've done for the hospital."

"Thanks," Dan replied. "It's been a challenge, but I've had a lot of fun watching everyone come together. The physicians and staff have a real passion about caring for this community. All I had to do was to get them to build on each other's strengths."

"Well that's no easy task, but somehow you pulled it off, and you actually made it look easy to those of us on the outside. I'm eager to learn how you did it." Kim was serious, and she had reason to be. East Towne Manufacturing was going to have to change if it was to remain competitive, and Kim knew that her job would be on the line if she didn't find ways to calm the staffing tensions while creating new products. As an engineer, she appreciated a smooth-running operation, but applying engineering principles to managing people and developing new products did not come easy for her.

They chatted about the challenges of managing in a changing environment and about business conditions in Newbury. Finally Sean strolled up and took a seat. "Hi guys. Sorry I'm late."

"Glad you could make it," replied Dan. "We were getting hungry." They scanned the menu and placed their orders. The mealtime conversation gave them a chance to get acquainted, learning about each other's family, educational backgrounds and interests. Dan listened carefully to what they were saying, but also to what they were not saying. He noticed that Kim was confident in her manner, but the confidence seemed to mask a deep concern about things she couldn't control. Sean was happy-go-lucky, but he seemed to be disappointed with the results of his career thus far. Dan gradually shifted the conversation to the Rotary Club.

"What do you guys make of the declining membership at the Rotary Club? I checked the numbers and it looks like we're down about 30% from where we were four years ago. What do you think is going on?"

Kim was the first to jump in. "Well for one thing, the meetings need to start and end on time. My time is precious, and so is everyone else's. The least they can do is show respect for our time." She shot a dark glance at Sean to see if he caught her veiled reprimand for being late for the lunch. Sean was thinking of other things.

"I'd like to see greater variety in the speakers and topics. We have heard plenty about the local economy and politics, but precious little to inspire humanitarian service or encourage the development of ethical standards in the community. Isn't that what a service club like Rotary is supposed to be about?"

"Those are both good thoughts," reflected Dan. "Let's keep this brainstorm going. The solutions are up to us, but we have lots of options. What else bothers you about the club?"

Kim was on a roll. "You know, I was pretty well-received as one of the first women in the club, but it's still basically an old-boys club. I feel like I'm tolerated, but I really wonder if I'll ever be treated as an equal. If that's how I feel after being a member for seven years, imagine how difficult it is for other capable women who might want to join. And another thing, we all pay dues, but when was the last time we all got a financial statement? How are the members supposed to trust the leaders if there is no transparency about how the money is being managed?"

Sean chimed in. "Yeah, I don't pay too much attention to the money, but we have had some pretty lavish parties. If we're a service club, shouldn't we be looking for ways to invest in our community instead? As far as not feeling like an equal, you're not alone on that one. I'm a small retailer, but sometimes I feel like a second-class citizen next to the bigger employers in town except when I'm with you guys. It's not exactly a welcoming feeling."

It was Dan's turn. "Those are all valid observations. I'm also curious about what we can learn from some of the people who have left. I'd like to know more about their reasons for leaving. The situation is unfortunate and difficult to measure except for the declining membership, but let's see what we could find out from those who dropped their membership. Maybe we can turn this around."

"You turned around the hospital," Kim piped in. "How did you do it and what can you teach us from your experience that might apply to the club?"

"Thanks for the compliment, but it was the result of a lot of people working together. I don't really believe I can take credit for it, but I've been watching carefully, and I think I've learned a few things that might help us."

"I'm all ears," quipped Sean. "What did you discover?"

"When I came to the hospital, there were two factions at odds with each other. One segment of the hospital community was quite contented with things the way they were and didn't see the need to change. They attributed the decline in market share to temporary conditions and rested on the fine traditions that brought us success in the past. The other faction sounded alarms about the future that seemed, well, alarmist, and their suggestions for change seemed reckless and exaggerated. Besides, some of the ideas were coming from people who didn't have a real good track record for following through."

"The division could be seen in each sub-group and department in the hospital. The staff, the physicians and the board seemed to be at each other's throats. What was worse, people on both sides weren't talking to each other to find solutions. The organization had survived a major change in Medicare financing as well as a shift from inpatient to outpatient services, and it still managed to hold its own against the bigger hospitals in the region. But there was a steady decline in our market share and it was getting more difficult to recruit and retain doctors and nurses."

"How did you get the two factions to work together?" Kim was taking notes.

"I looked carefully at both perspectives and realized that each faction had something valuable to offer. If they worked together, they would be able to achieve much more than if they didn't cooperate. They each represented a set of business strategies that we should pay attention to."

Dan began to draw a diagram on his notepad. He drew a large block arrow rising from the lower-left quadrant to the upper right center of the page as he continued. "The first group was very **systematic**. They focused on studying historical data and current research in medicine, and relied heavily on what worked in the past when it came to business decisions. Then they refined those systems of doing things so the hospital could reduce its costs and build on its reputation.

"One example was the way the hospital improved its emergency department. Complaints about waiting times were coming from all directions, so the staff and physicians tracked the actual waiting times, studied the causes for delays, researched what other hospitals were doing to reduce bottlenecks, and came up with a list of recommendations.

After a few modifications to the facility, the paperwork process, and some staff retraining, the waiting time dropped 40% in six months. They had that department running like a machine. One of my vice presidents described them as having 'elegant systems,' which I think was pretty accurate. They made a difficult process look easy, and improved customer satisfaction AND quality of care in the process."

Dan wrote "Elegant Systems" under the block arrow. Then he drew another block arrow to mirror the first one as he continued.

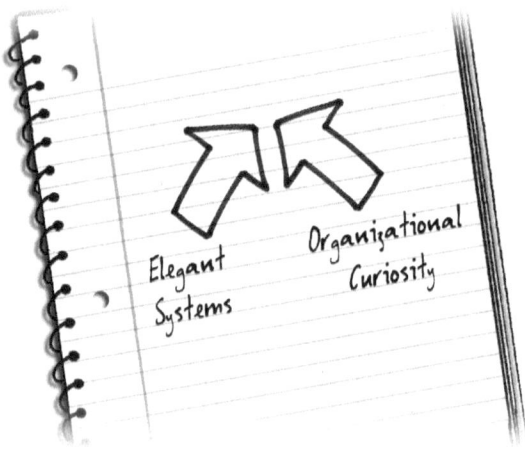

"But while the improvements in the Emergency Department were going on, the other faction was being critical of the resources we were consuming in the process. They pointed out that the population growth in the community was strongest in the north part of town rather than in the south, where the hospital is located. They suggested that if we really wanted to give people access to us, we should have an urgent care center where the growth is happening. They were paying attention to market changes and campaigned for new facilities that could meet the changing needs of our community.

"But wouldn't it have been too expensive to develop a new facility at the same time you improved the capacity of your emergency department?" Sean was listening intently.

"It was expensive, but the idea was tested by financial wizards on the team, who were mostly systematic types. They examined various models and concluded that if we used the same techniques developed by the emergency department to streamline patient flow, we could start with a smaller facility on the north side and still operate with a positive margin. The originators of the idea then took it a step further. They compared the waiting times at competitors on the north side and concluded that we'd have a strategic advantage with our prompt response-time model."

Kim glanced at Sean with an inquisitive smile. "So what did you call the second group?"

"We called them curious," replied Dan, "because they were asking questions that the systematic people weren't thinking about." He wrote "Organizational Curiosity" under the second block arrow.

Dan enjoyed the chance to talk about the turnaround at the hospital, but he wasn't sure how relevant his experience would be for other organizations, including the Rotary Club. He was about to find out.

Dan Introduces the Model

"So if I understand the diagram correctly," Sean observed, "you made better decisions and got better results when these two approaches joined forces."

"That's right. In fact, once we understood these two approaches better, we were able to construct a model that guided us in other decision-making processes. But I'm getting ahead of myself."

"Yes, you are," Kim said, leaning forward. "I'd like to hear more about these two approaches, systems elegance and organizational curiosity. How did you define them? I don't think I've ever heard those terms in the business literature."

"We've been dissecting the changes that took place at Community Hospital over the past eight years, in part because we want to learn from the experience so we can continue to improve, and in part because other hospitals are asking us how we did it. We're still in the early stages of our reflection, but I'll tell you what we understand at this point.

Elegant systems allow organizations to get consistent positive results from routine processes. Some of our processes are very complex and essential for good patient care, but by systematically refining them, we improved patient care AND reduced our costs. Elegant systems make difficult tasks appear easy. Think of two different games on ice. We asked ourselves what we wanted our work to look like: a rough-and-tumble hockey game or figure skating. We chose the elegance of figure skating."

Dan continued, "Elegant systems keep the organization focused on moving people, equipment and inventory quickly and smoothly, consistently raising the quality of the service while lowering the cost, and thereby producing excellent value. We try to stay fluid and flexible so we can adapt to changes in our market."

"I think I'm getting it," Kim said. "In my business, we're always trying to increase the speed of production, but sometimes quality suffers and the result can hardly be described as elegant. I guess we're more like a hockey team. What are some examples of elegant systems at the hospital?"

"We use checklists to prepare the surgical suites for each case. Medication delivery systems have various safeguards, including making sure we have different colored containers for different doses of some of the most potent pharmaceuticals to avoid medication errors, and we use barcodes to track inventory of every supply item in the hospital so we can capture charges appropriately and keep just the right amount of inventory on hand."

"I could benefit from better inventory control systems," Sean piped in. "When I get overstocked and have to put items in the discount bin to move them, it really eats up my profit margin. But tell us more about organizational curiosity. That's not a term we hear at trade shows or business conferences either."

"**Organizational curiosity** is a quality of the culture in an organization. It can be described as made up of at least three different strategies. First, it's the ability to *anticipate how the market is changing* and to position the organization to meet those new expectations," continued Dan. "Every manager has to be a futurist to some degree, keeping an eye on trends in the industry, in the community, and in the dynamics of the organization. In the hospital, for example, we have to be attuned to the aging of our physicians as well as to the demographic shifts in our community. Physician recruitment is a long and complex process, so we have to anticipate the community's needs well in advance, and provide opportunities for young physicians to learn about their practice options in Newbury as they are making their career decisions rather than wait until our existing docs announce their retirement plans.

"The second part of being a curious organization is paying attention to your staff in fresh ways. You probably recognize the term 'right-sizing' as a euphemism for 'down-sizing,' right? Well we coined a different term: *'right-jobbing'* which means that we hire people to do what they *love* to do. We've become quite good about placing people on the basis of their natural skills and their passions, more than relying on their experience. We know that when people enjoy their work, they produce at higher levels and they get along with others who also enjoy their work. Teamwork isn't just a slogan with us. It's a way of life because we place people with co-workers that complement each other's skills and passions."

"Right-jobbing. Fascinating." Kim was taking it all in.

"Curiosity is also about *abandoning ideas* that are no longer valid and being *early adopters* of new technology and business concepts that can help the organization adapt to changing market expectations. It's easy to maintain old ways of doing things without questioning them in most organizations, but we invite everyone – patients, staff, vendors and visitors to constantly critique everything we do, knowing that those who are impacted by our ways of doing things are in the best position to tell us how to improve." Dan was relaxed as he described the hospital management's openness to critique.

Kim became a bit uncomfortable as she thought about what might happen at East Towne Manufacturing if she were as open as that. She was usually the one to initiate changes based on her personal observations as the CEO, but she paused as she considered the impact of asking her machine tool operators and her customers for ideas about better ways of doing things. "In a way, it would make my job easier to be so transparent because others can see things that I can't see, but doesn't it drive you crazy to have everyone trying to tell you how to do your job?"

Sean spoke up before Dan could answer. "The old adage in retailing is that 'the customer is always right,' and in my experience, that makes good sense. But I can also see the value of getting input from my staff and my suppliers. We all have biases that cloud our imagination from time to time, and getting multiple perspectives can really open up opportunities for new products and better ways of delivering them. I'm already a big fan of organizational curiosity."

"Then I think you'll both appreciate the model we came up with for putting it all together." Dan drew another diagram, and this time he asked the waitress for some crayons she kept to entertain her youngest customers while they waited for their food. "We call it the Star Performance Model." He made a triangle with two crisscrossed lines and colored each quadrant a different color.

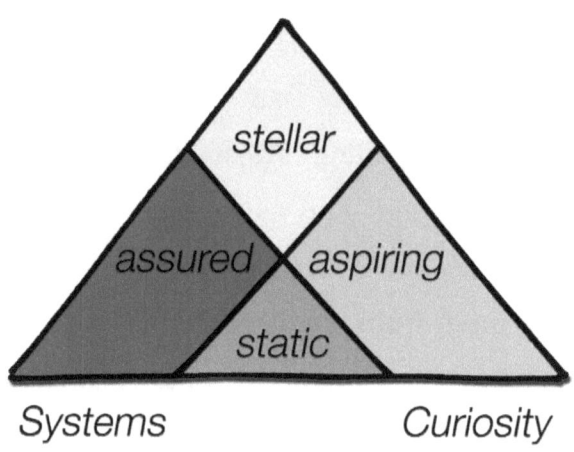

"We decided to assess the performance in each department using the concepts of systems elegance and organizational curiosity," Dan continued as he drew. "Some departments had become quite systematic over the years. It was not uncommon for us to hear things like, 'We've always done it that way before' in those departments. We labeled them Assured Performers." He wrote "assured" in the lower left quadrant that had been colored blue.

"Other departments were innovative, but not very systematic, and they usually had persistent budget problems as a result. We called them Aspiring Performers." Dan jotted "aspiring" in the lower right yellow quadrant.

"But there were examples in most departments of at least moments when they put it all together – both elegant systems and organizational curiosity – to achieve Stellar Performance." He wrote "stellar" in the top green block. "We have several stories about exceptional service, process improvements and financial turnarounds throughout the hospital." Dan smiled as he remembered some of his star employees and departments. They were ordinary people who had accomplished extraordinary results.

"What about the red block at the bottom?" asked Sean.

"We decided to call them Static Performers because they were neither systematic nor curious, and they weren't going anywhere. They were stuck in their ways. They were static." He wrote "static" in the uninviting red block.

"This is very interesting," commented Kim. "How did you use the model?"

"We simply explained elegant systems and organizational curiosity to the department managers just like I explained it to you, and then we asked them where they thought they were on the model. Most of them knew right away."

"And I can see where the Rotary Club is," Sean exclaimed. "We're assured because we aren't paying attention to the kinds of programming that members want, and that's why so many have left."

"I am thinking that we are aspiring," Kim chimed in. "If we were systematic, we'd start and end on time and be more transparent with the finances."

"I think you're both right." Dan was smiling. "That's one of the beauties of this model. When you assess your current performance on any particular topic, you immediately get a sense about what it will take to become a stellar performer on that issue. And there are plenty of issues to focus on."

As the model began to sink in, each one around the table got a sense about what should happen next for the Rotary Club and what their individual role should be. Sean was the first to volunteer.

"I'd like to explore fresh ideas about speakers and topics for our weekly meetings. Some of my friends have some pretty unique hobbies, and maybe we can tap a few neighboring clubs for ideas that were big hits at their meetings."

"Good idea," Kim replied, "and I'd like to be the timekeeper for the meetings as well as dig into the financial picture. Maybe a little consistency will encourage some of the members we've lost to return."

"Those are both great ideas," Dan nodded. "I think we should all do one more thing before we meet again next week. Let's talk to members that have left in the past two years to find out what they can tell us about improving the club." Kim and Sean enthusiastically endorsed Dan's idea and they split up the list of past members to follow up with.

As they left the restaurant, Dan felt hopeful. "Maybe the lessons we've learned through the hospital turnaround are valuable for the whole community," he thought.

The Club Catches On

The first meeting of the Rotary Club under the leadership of the new officers had a distinctly different tone. The meeting started promptly on time even though about a quarter of the members straggled in late. Kim sat near the back of the room and served as Dan's timekeeper, letting him know with hand signals when it was time to introduce the speaker, and giving the speaker a five-minute notice when the meeting was to conclude.

Sean had arranged a presentation by a local physician who was also a professional ventriloquist, and the club enjoyed a humorous education about the long term effects of a sedentary lifestyle. Dan overheard comments from the members as they left about the memorable insights gained, and one of the oldest members said, "I hope you get more programs like that one."

When the Rotary Club officers met for lunch again, they were all a few minutes early, and everyone was smiling.

"I can't wait to tell you what I've been learning from former members who left the club," Sean exclaimed. "I talked to five people and they were pretty consistent in describing the club as boring and uninspiring. But when I told them about last week's presentation, most of them perked up. I think we have a good chance of getting some of them back if we continue to attract programs like that."

Kim agreed. "I'm hearing the same kind of things. In fact, it surprised me a little that most people mentioned the programming first. Some also talked about the lack of discipline about meeting times, but it was more of a minor irritant than a driving reason for them to quit the club. But I also heard that ideas for community service projects were being squelched, and that really concerns me. If we're going to be a relevant community service club, we need to act on those ideas and stimulate more suggestions, not discourage them."

Dan nodded. "I also heard a lot about the desire to make a difference in the community. It seems to me that there are some generous people in this town that are looking for an organization like the Rotary Club to channel their efforts for the benefit of the whole community. And some of those who left would come back if we provide a way for their ideas and energies to be put into action. I think our club has been suffering mostly from a lack of organizational curiosity."

"I'm curious," said Kim, "why most people seemed to focus on programming and service ideas – the curiosity issues – rather than on the more systematic issues like the starting and ending times and the financial transparency."

"Well, let's think about that," replied Dan. "Do you think improving systems might have the same impact as improving organizational curiosity?"

Sean responded. "Not according to the people I talked with. Sure, they were irritated by the lack of discipline at the meetings, but they were passionate when they talked about the need for better programming, and it sounds like the people you both talked with were also passionate about service projects. I think we'd have to make changes in those areas first to win them back and to attract new members."

"I agree," Dan nodded. "If the club is going to become a star performer, I think we'll have to start with improving the club's curiosity. That's what our research with former members seems to be telling us, and if a few changes in programming and community service are effective, the club is most likely to grow again.

And isn't that the kind of performance we're looking for?"

Kim was scribbling something on a napkin. "As an engineer, I think mathematically," she said as she showed them her napkin. "Maybe there's an algebraic formula to describe the relationship between systems and curiosity. What do you think?"

The napkin had a strange formula written on it:

$$P = s(c^2)$$

"Math wasn't my strongest subject," replied Sean. "Can you interpret this?"

"Sure," said Kim. "P equals s-c squared means that performance improves when you make changes to both systems and curiosity, but they're not equal. Improving organizational curiosity will have an exponential impact on performance compared to improving systems."

Sean was scratching his head. "Does that mean that we should skip improving systems and concentrate on improving the programming and service projects?"

"No, I don't think so," replied Kim. "It just means that we're more likely to draw former members back and attract new members to the club by doing what they value most. They have told us to make the meetings interesting and sponsor service projects that will improve the community. We can refine the systems later."

"That's very interesting," commented Dan, "and you know, it makes a lot of sense. In fact, I can see how we applied this formula in the hospital without even realizing it. Some of our systems problems required significant investments in facilities and equipment to solve. I'm glad we first concentrated on what the market was expecting of us before we spent a lot of time and money improving those systems. We invested discussion time and market research in curiosity things first, and that's when we concluded that we should have a presence on the north side of town. If we had made major investments in our south-side emergency department without understanding how the market was changing, we might not have had enough capital left to put an urgent care center where the market wanted us to be. We invested in raising our organizational curiosity before we put real money into the facilities and equipment. I guess we knew intuitively that curiosity would have an exponential impact on our performance."

"And if this formula is correct," replied Kim, "our efforts at improving programs and service projects in the club will impact our membership growth more than improving the timing and finances."

"Yes, but let's not forget those systems issues," said Sean. "What did you find out about our financial condition?" Dan and Kim were mildly surprised to hear Sean call attention to systems.

Kim produced financial reports to share with Sean and Dan. "We're in reasonable shape," she said, "but when I talked with the former treasurer, he indicated that he just never got around to sharing the information with the membership because he didn't think it was important. I think we owe them an update, and we can use this report to point out that we haven't spent much on community service projects for a long time. That might help to stimulate some ideas and motivation for new projects."

"I can also bring in speakers from some of the local non-profit agencies," said Sean. "There are plenty of needs right under our noses, and the directors at those agencies will be happy to tell us about them. Maybe I'll start with the director at the United Way. I've known Amy for the past few years. She's a fireball. I'm sure she'll have an interesting presentation."

"Sounds good," said Dan. "Let's keep this ball rolling. I'm eager to see what happens."

"You know, I've always heard that 'curiosity kills the cat,'" said Sean, "but it looks to me like curiosity keeps the cat alive."

As they paid for lunch and returned to their offices, the three sensed that they were part of a movement that was bigger than all of them put together. They each had a sense of deep satisfaction that the club – and the community – were about to take off. But they couldn't have imagined the impact they were about to witness.

The Club Wakes Up

Over the next several weeks, the Rotary Club became the talk of the town. About half of the members that had left in the past two years returned, and a few more newcomers joined as well. Sean had no trouble lining up interesting speakers and Kim made sure the meeting schedule respected everyone's time. Sharing the financial statements had the impact the leaders hoped for, and several promising ideas for service projects started to surface from even some of the most sedentary members.

Soon there were more than a dozen service project ideas ranging from work projects like renovating a run-down school playground to more passive projects like sponsoring an international exchange student. A committee was set up to evaluate the projects and organize teams to carry them out. Donations started to pour in to support the projects from members who hadn't given much in the past, and there was a good turnout for the first Saturday workday, installing new playground toys at Calder Elementary School.

The club officers picked up compliments from unlikely corners of the community. Mrs. Wilson's second grade class at Calder Elementary School sent a big drawing they had made of the new playground. The poster had a big "Thank you" at the bottom and was signed with the personal touch of each student.

Kim overheard a conversation at the salon one Saturday about the changes in the community. The wife of a Lions Club member was asking the wife of a Rotarian about the flurry of activity she had seen. The community spirit was becoming contagious.

Even St. Paul's Catholic Church got into the act. Father Clooney asked to join the club after hearing about service projects the club sponsored to clean up the yards of three of his elderly parishioners. Shortly after joining, he pulled Dan aside after one of the meetings to thank him for his leadership. "Joining the club has really helped me see the community in a new light," he said. "There are so many needs right under our noses, but there are also untapped resources ready to pitch in. We're all connected, aren't we?" Dan nodded with a broad smile. He wondered whether Father Clooney would be interested in becoming an officer for the club someday.

The Rotary Club was becoming a Stellar Performer.

Sean's Hallmark

But the Rotary Club wasn't the only organization experiencing a renaissance. Sean began to think about how the Stellar Performance Model could impact his Hallmark store. He recognized himself as an aspiring performer. He was always intrigued with ideas for new products, but had a difficult time controlling his inventory and keeping costs under control. His wife, Kathy, did the books for the store, and she was a good judge of people. When she suggested that Ingrid, Sean's employee of eight years, seemed to have good skills at managing information, Sean decided to try some improvements. He asked Ingrid to evaluate methods for tracking inventory and to figure out which products were most profitable. She jumped at the opportunity as if she had been waiting for the chance to use her skills. Within a week she approached Sean with recommendations for using barcodes to monitor product turnover and spreadsheets to evaluate the profitability of each item in the store. She pointed out that his entire stock turned over about two times per year, but that by using the barcode inventory control system, he could increase the turnover to at least three times per year, resulting in more than enough profits to pay for the technology required to implement the barcode system. Sean used Ingrid's analysis to convince his banker to give him a loan for the new barcode equipment, and then he watched as the turnover rate exceeded Ingrid's projection. With less cash tied up in inventory, he had no trouble paying the loan on time.

Ingrid also monitored the profitability of each item and found that Sean had a habit of discontinuing the most profitable lines. When she brought him her analysis, he was amazed. He acknowledged that he often got bored with some of those product lines and assumed that since he was bored with them, his customers must be also. Together they decided to bring a few of the most profitable products back and to monitor the sales rates systematically rather than rely on Sean's intuition.

Kathy was the first to notice the impact of these changes. The profits at the store began to soar. Sean decided to make a few long-overdue improvements like replacing the worn carpeting and improving the lighting to brighter, more energy-efficient fixtures. He also negotiated a favorable advertising contract with the local newspaper, and the traffic in the store seemed to increase along with the sales volume and profitability.

Sean's Hallmark was becoming a Stellar Performer.

East Towne Manufacturing

Kim was also applying the Stellar Performance Model at East Towne Manufacturing. She thought about what the club leaders had learned by talking with former members and decided to contact every customer served by East Towne in the past two years. She prepared a simple easy-to-complete survey for her clients, and offered a small gift card to a national office supply chain to everyone who responded.

The survey results were astonishing. Kim learned about concerns ranging from product quality to the rudeness of sales staff. When she shared the results with her supervisors, she also heard their concerns about staffing levels and equipment breakdowns. She realized that it was time to share the Stellar Performance Model with everyone at East Towne Manufacturing.

She began with her supervisors. She showed them the model and defined systems elegance and organizational curiosity in terms that made sense to their working environment. Then she asked them to describe where they thought the company was on the model. The majority recognized that East Towne Manufacturing was an assured performer and they could see that they needed to improve the organization's curiosity to become a stellar performer.

The supervisors shared the model with their front-line teams and the ideas for improvements began to flow. Most of the ideas had to do with processes rather than equipment, and those that could be implemented without cost were put in place immediately. One of the forklift drivers seemed to be particularly creative, and he produced a dozen suggestions that Kim estimated saved the company at least $100,000 per year. She made sure he got recognized at the next staff meeting, and his next paycheck had an appropriate bonus in it as well. Inspired by his ingenuity, others shared their ideas for process improvements more freely, and the entire organization began to sparkle.

Kim decided to make the customer surveys a regular feature and she was soon able to monitor the progress based on the results. She produced graphs showing the improvements and posted them in the employee lunch room in addition to sharing them at her regular meetings with supervisors. The financial results came later, as though they were a byproduct of the changes in organizational curiosity.

East Towne Manufacturing was becoming a Stellar Performer.

Newbury

Other business and civic leaders started to notice the subtle changes taking place at Sean's Hallmark and East Towne Manufacturing as well as at Community Hospital and the Rotary Club. The three leaders received compliments regularly and used those occasions to share the Stellar Performance Model with others. The impact began to ripple throughout the community.

The city manager introduced the model at a planning retreat for the city council, stimulating ideas for improvements to the public works department. The council quickly realized that they had antiquated equipment for street repairs. Their systems, they thought, had worked just fine for years. But they discovered that the equipment – as well as the old engineering technologies for resurfacing streets – resulted in repairs that did not hold up as well as repairs that were possible from newer equipment and technology. When they compared the current costs of street repairs with the projected costs of less frequent, more durable repairs with new equipment, they found the justification for investing in better technology – and better streets.

The superintendent of public schools studied the model for ideas about improving communications with parents. She had relied on a personal open-door policy, public media, and periodic public meetings to keep parents informed of major changes in the school system. Being open to new ideas, she had thought, was enough. The Stellar Performance Model showed her that there was room for improvement in being consistent and systematic in communications – in both directions. As a result, she publicized a telephone hotline and email address for parents to voice their concerns, with the promise of a staff response in 24 hours or less. She quickly discovered that responding to small concerns early headed off bigger concerns down the road. As she became more systematic with communications, she found parents became more committed to the educational process and to communicating with their kids' teachers.

The town of Newbury was becoming a Stellar Performer.

Part 2: The Stellar Performance Model

About The Stellar Performance Model

The Stellar Performance Model is like many other models in that it is a metaphor for how things work. It describes in a simple manner how the best organizations thrive, based on simple observation and intuition. It is intended to stimulate thinking about the future of organizations and inspire people to build on complementary strengths to improve their organizations and communities.

But there is also something unique about the Stellar Performance Model. I have introduced the model to people in developing countries around the world, and the results have been consistently fascinating to watch. People understand the model almost immediately. Their eyes light up. It is both intuitive and informative. When I have returned to the audiences in some of those developing countries, I have heard stories about how managers have used the model to improve their organizations and how they have shared the model with others.

I have had the pleasure of serving as an advisor and mentor to a medical center in Romania for over a decade. When I began, the country was slowly gaining an awareness of free-market economic dynamics. The clinic leaders showed excellent curiosity about how to develop and manage a high-quality service, but they had no examples to work from. They had ideas, but lacked systems to implement their ideas.

I began by helping them articulate what they wanted to accomplish. They described an outpatient center known for its high medical quality and solid business integrity, which was rare for the country at that time. That image represented stellar performance to them.

Then we talked about what patients wanted when they sought medical care (or what patients were curious about). They talked about respect, cleanliness, reliability and value. The clinic leaders envisioned that people would gladly pay out-of-pocket for qualities they couldn't get in the government-run clinics.

After we reached an understanding of the qualities people valued, we turned to systems that would be required to meet – and exceed – their expectations. We focused on clean and bright facilities, state-of-the-art equipment, staff attitudes and education, and the financial policies to keep the organization growing.

The Dr. Luca Medical Center has consistently grown through continuous improvement to become a shining example for Eastern Europe, and has served as an inspiration to health care leaders in Asia, Africa and Latin America.

Why the Model Works

One explanation for why the Stellar Performance Model seems to resonate intuitively is because it reflects the anatomical construction of our brains and the neurological relationship between the two hemispheres. Psychobiologist Roger Sperry won the Nobel Prize in 1981 for his discovery of how the mind functions in balance, the left brain controlling organizational and structural tasks while the right brain controls the emotive and creative roles. The fibers that bind the two sides, called the *corpus callosum*, unite the efforts of both hemispheres to achieve balanced performance.

Think of systems elegance and organizational curiosity in parallel terms.

System Elegance is to Organizational Curiosity as:

Engineering	is to	Imagination
Action		Idea
Hand		Head
Muscle		Mind
Methods		Culture
Left Brain		Right Brain

Another reason the model is effective is that it simplifies the complex process of organizational change and makes it attainable for everyone. If you can identify your current position in the model, you can immediately get a sense about what is needed to improve the organization. Assured performers need to raise their curiosity and aspiring performers need to invest in their systems. The next steps will depend on the unique circumstances of the organization, but almost every reader can fill in

the blanks about what some of those next steps
might need to be.

Other Key Observations

Three more observations are critical to applying the Stellar Performance Model. First, it is important to recognize that organizational performance requires constant adaptation and change. Market dynamics are constantly evolving, such that the efforts required for stellar performance next year will be different than the efforts required this year. The bar is always being raised, which is why organizational curiosity needs to constantly re-define what it means to be successful.

The second observation is that stellar performers are never satisfied. Even when they are at the top of their game, they are *constructively discontented,* looking for the next improvements they can make to stay at the top of their game. They don't have time for arrogance or hubris because they understand that the market is constantly changing and competitors are always on the move as well.

Stellar performers enjoy the process of improvement, but when they accomplish one project, they are humble about their achievements and already looking for the next challenge. It is as though they are saying, "That was fun. Now what can we do for an encore?"

Static performers offer a dramatic contrast to stellar performers. They are neither curious nor systematic and their organizations are in serious trouble. You would think that they would be concerned. It is more likely, however, that they will be oblivious to changes in their industry or their business, and they will be heading for obsolescence unless they get a wake-up call soon. As the bar is rising for stellar performers, the sun is setting for static performers.

Third, while every organization may aspire to be a stellar performer in every area, it is more likely to have moments of stellar performance in different departments or functions at different times rather than to be at the top of their game in every area every day. Maybe the personnel functions are doing well, but the manufacturing process is a bit stagnant. Perhaps the cost control efforts are effective but the planning efforts are unimaginative. Build on the successes within the organization and let the Stellar Performance Model become contagious. When continuous improvements build on each other, the organization develops a virtuous cycle toward stellar performance.

What the Model Means for Marketers

The sales process can be very challenging, even under the best of circumstances. Sales people have to face a lot of rejection along the way to finding an accepting audience. The Stellar Performance Model may be helpful, however, to focus sales efforts in directions that minimize resistance.

Organizations that have a high degree of curiosity are likely to be early adopters of new technology and ideas that can impact their future, so products and services that are on the cutting edge are likely to find a higher rate of acceptance with curious organizations. Likewise, systems-oriented companies will be on the lookout for products and services that help them streamline their systems so they can produce more output with less input.

Sales efforts are more likely to be effective if you can segment the market into performance types, using the Stellar Performance Model. If your product or service represents a new technology or idea, you are more likely to find interested audiences in aspiring performance organizations and resistance in assured performers. Conversely, if your product represents a refinement of old technology that can streamline existing processes, you will be more likely to find a welcoming audience with systematic assured performers than with aspiring performers.

Identifying which segment each organization is in becomes the next challenge, but you can find clues by asking questions like these:

1. Which organizations have experienced slow but steady growth? (assured)
2. Which managers are eager to try anything? (aspiring)
3. Which companies consistently ask for input? (aspiring)

4. Which organizations have products that are staples or market leaders? (assured)

Generally speaking, younger organizations are more likely to be curious than older, more established companies, but every organization has the potential to become a stellar performer.

The performance type of the target organization can also give sales staff clues about what features and benefits to emphasize. Aspiring performers are likely to be more interested in the hope and promise of cutting edge technologies whereas assured performers may be looking for cost savings that result from improved systems. Sales presentations that speak to the audience are less likely to face resistance.

Personal Development

The Stellar Performance Model was originally designed by observing organizations, but it can also help individuals find focus for their careers and advance their skills. The model can also help you learn to work with complementary teams to gain the opportunity for exponential achievement.

Nobel Prize-winner Roger Sperry identified that we each have a natural dominance in either the right or left hemisphere of our brain. Recognizing our own natural ways of thinking opens the door to learning how to collaborate. Right-brained people need to work with left-brained thinkers, and *vice versa*. By working with those who think in complementary patterns, we can accelerate our joint achievements.

Self-knowledge also helps us understand the kinds of people we should surround ourselves with. A right-brain dominant manager would do well to have left-brain dominant colleagues to temper his creativity and test his ideas before taking on significantly risky new ventures. A left-brained executive should give permission to right-brained colleagues to challenge his systematic thinking and keep an eye out for fresh ideas.

Our educational system seems to be geared toward left-brain dominance. By the time we get through college, we have been exposed to some 2,600 tests, quizzes and exams that encourage us to come up with a single right answer. Those with left-brain dominance usually do well in that kind of environment while the right-brained students are usually looking for multiple right answers and often find themselves either bored or easily distracted in a typical classroom environment. Entrepreneurs and inventors often begin as right-brained students, but they need the left-brained accountants and engineers to provide sufficient structure to keep their newfound organizations going. By working together, they can each achieve stellar performance both personally and professionally.

Steve Jobs at Apple Computer is a classic example. His legendary knack for designing visionary products has fueled the imagination of engineers at Apple and warmed the hearts of Mac, iPod and iPhone users worldwide. He has clearly assembled a team of systematic implementers to complement the creativity that flows through Apple as smoothly as Friday-afternoon beer.

How to Use the Model in Your Organization

The Stellar Performance Model can be useful for both individual and organizational development. It can be explained in relatively simple, easy-to-understand terms in as little as 15 minutes, and it can serve as the basis for assessing, improving or planning any organization. To make it relevant, begin by asking where your organization might be on the model right now. Then delve deeper into your systems elegance and organizational curiosity with questions like these, tailored to your particular industry and situation:

- "How can we discern what our customers will expect of us next year?"
- "Who in our organization are the best ones to work on (a specific) problem?"
- "What slows us down or limits our ability to delight the people we serve?"
- "Why do we have (particular) recurring issues?"

The discussions that flow out of these questions and others like them will offer guidance for refining your operations, provide clues about new products and services worthy of consideration, and increase the likelihood of raising your profitability and market share.